What pe
Camille D

Whether she's

and happy daughters, or tearing it up on the dance floor, Camille practices happiness every day. Things may not always go as planned, but Camille shares personal insights and life lessons she has used to take charge of her own happiness. Readers will gain positive practices they can incorporate into their own lives from this book.

-Wendy Reed

I have had a wonderful coaching experience with Camille Diaz. She has an uncanny way of seeing the big picture when I cannot and she offers priceless advice and perspective to run my real estate business successfully. I look forward to my coaching sessions with her because I know once the session is complete I will have a renewed energy and new ideas to tackle my obstacles.

-Chandra Hall

You have a healing product, and I told you many of my stories... because of your book. I am thrilled to know you. I think your book is exciting. I was honored to read it.

-Julie Tattershall

I was fortunate to meet Camille three years ago. Her advice saved my marriage, her advice and skills saved my business. She is a top notch quality person, personally (I know her family) and professionally, she changed the way I thought about myself, my business and others. She totally changed my image. I hope you're fortunate enough to read her book and meet her in person.

-Gunner Peterson

Camille makes it her personal mission and responsibility to make others a success. From strategizing to providing constructive criticism, she takes her wealth of knowledge from operating her own successful business and imparts self-confidence and positivity into those she coaches.

-Andi McDaniel

For most of my 68 years I've been self-conscious of my body image. Through her amazing self-confidence, Camille has taught me to be comfortable in my own skin… now I can even, "Dance like no one is watching!"

-Roberta Houston

Have you ever had one of those people in your life who comes and goes every few years? A high school friend you haven't seen for six years and suddenly you pick up exactly where you left off? Let me tell you, Camille is that person... she is this way with everyone and it doesn't matter how long it's been since you've seen her! She will always pick up right where you left off. You can look into her eyes and know she is authentic, the real deal, a person with a good heart. Camille puts a positive spin on everything and puts family and friends first. She is certainly not afraid of swimming in the deep end.

-Heather Corbit

I read it! It's really cool! I liked how you laid out a guideline to help people sort out how to get on track.

-Elizabeth Bowman

Camille has a way of encouraging motivation with a soft and wise approach that praises much poise. As her employee, I felt comfortable and I continue to use the tools she taught me in dance, business, and personal affairs. I regard her with an enormous amount of respect and see her as a strong, powerful, female role model in my life.

-Smidge Isgrig

In times of stress and indecision I turn to Camille. It is easy for me to get lost in the rabbit holes in my head and I often need help climbing out and seeing things clearly. Camille has a knack for telling me exactly what I need to hear to sort myself out. She doesn't give me orders, but gives me the confidence to trust myself and my decisions. Especially when it comes to following my dreams. Even those dreams which don't follow a traditional path or have an obvious revenue stream. She can make me feel confident in my own ideas in less than three sentences. Often when feeling lost I ask myself 'what would Camille tell me' or 'how would Camille approach this' and that helps tremendously. She truly helps me cut through the chaos in my life, and in my head, so I can move forward towards success.

-Rosemma Strombom

The Shake Up

Misfit to Best Fit in 30 Days

By

Camille Diaz

HOLLY -
ENJOY THE
JOURNEY.
- CAMILLE
2017.10.31

© Copyright 2017, Camille Diaz

All Rights Reserved

No part of this book may be reproduced, stored in a retrieval system, or transmitted by any means, electronic, mechanical, photocopying, recording, or otherwise, without written permission from the author.

ISBN: 978-1-63302-072-6

Disclaimer

The information contained in this book is intended as reference material only. It is not to be used as a substitute for professional advice by legal, medical, financial, business, spiritual, or other qualified professionals. It is your responsibility to practice due diligence and seek independent professional guidance in these matters. All decisions in these areas and beyond are exclusively yours; your decisions and your actions regarding them are your sole responsibility.

Dedication

Dedicated to John Reader Johnson who lives on as a voice of wisdom inside my head.

And to all those who are willing to embrace change, choose happiness, and enjoy this fleeting adventure called life.

Acknowledgements

Special thanks to Tyler Strombom, Julie Tattershall, Rosemma Strombom, and especially my husband, Anthony Diaz. Without your encouragement and honest feedback, I wouldn't have pushed myself so far. Sincere gratitude to all those who have believed in me and supported me throughout this journey. Knowing you have my back gives me strength to move forward.

Table of Contents

Author's Note

Dear Reader,

Welcome to *The Shake Up*. I created this book for people who want to calm the chaos in their lives, find their purpose, and follow their dreams. The techniques I reveal here are the same ones I teach my coaching clients. The same ones I have learned through years of trial and error in my own life and in my businesses. The same ones which helped me and my clients learn to trust our intuition and make decisions from a place of clarity and understanding rather than a place of frustration and desperation.

I've written this book as a 30-day guide. Each day has a short story, guidance and strategies from me, and an activity for you. You can make your way through the book and get on a path toward changing your life in just a few minutes a day. My goal is to help you be the best you, to help you create a strategy to reduce stress and streamline your life. I want you to create a better work-life balance for yourself, accept yourself, feel happier, and have the courage to make changes. If you're ready to break out of your current habits and foster an opportunity for change, keep reading, and continue *The Shake Up*.

Hugs,

-Camille

Ready. Set. Go.

Ever feel like things just aren't going your way? Feel like that most of the time? I did. It seemed no matter how hard I worked I was always behind. No matter how much I tried to fit in I felt out of place. I figured out how to tame my crazy hair, how to say the right words, how to laugh at the right times, and how to get the work done, but somehow my life just wasn't coming together. I did not feel as happy, satisfied, or as secure as I wanted to feel. When my third small business failed miserably I was devastated. I spent a month in bed sleeping, eating, and binge watching Netflix. When I finally got out of there I realized I had gained more than 10 pounds, I had gained a new perspective. I knew what I needed to do and learned what was missing in my life. The problem was not everyone else, it was me. I figured out why I felt unfulfilled and what was required for my happiness. Here, I will share those revelations with you so you too can find your own inner peace.

I had spent far too much time working towards a dream which was not my own. I was focusing on what was important to others instead of what was truly important to me. When I refocused my life and energy toward my own goals, and started accepting my strengths and weaknesses, my life turned around. I became less stressed and much happier, as did those around me.

This book contains stories paired with my ideas and suggestions for shaking up your life and deciding where you want to go. Some of these stories are real, some are half-real, and others are completely made up. In all cases, the names have been changed to protect the innocent, the apathetic, and the guilty. Along with each day of stories I have included an activity called a "Shake-Up." The Shake-Ups are a variety of activities designed to help you practice the strategies being discussed after each story. The goal is to help you change your old routine or try something new. The way I see it, if you don't do anything different, nothing will change.

Making small changes can help us break out of old habits and create better ones if we choose. I've included descriptions and tips; however, the Shake-Ups are open to interpretation. I encourage you to be creative because the point is to shake up your life and consider situations from a different angle, not simply follow along.

The 30 days are broken up into six parts. Each part focuses on one of my core concepts for change: Stand Down, Tune In, Let Go, Look Inside, Do Better, and Stand Up. More about each of those later. At the end of each of the six parts, you will need to write a little. It doesn't matter if you write by hand or type. Be sure to use a separate sheet of paper or move to the next page in your document for each day's entry. I like the physical act of writing important things down because it helps me remember, so I will be referring to writing throughout the book. There is a custom PDF form with all the pages you will need. If you would like a free copy you can download it from my website, TheShakeUpBook.com. Once you have it you can print and hand write, or save it to your computer and fill it in there. Feel free to use any format which works for you as long as it's not the old "I'll just remember this" format. We both know that method doesn't work! When you are done, save your lists where you will be able to find them and do not open them until told to do so later on in the book.

If you don't have time to complete one chapter a day for 30 days straight, no sweat. This is not an ab challenge and the 30 days do not have to be done without breaks. Simply finish one day and go on to the next as soon as you are ready. If you want to stay on a schedule but take a break on weekends, try stretching the program to six weeks by doing one part per week. Each day is meant to give you a concept to consider and a Shake-Up to conquer, so avoid rushing ahead and trying to complete multiple days at once. Enjoy the journey.

Part 1

Stand Down

To make changes in your life you must be ready and willing. For some, a major life event like a move to a new city or the birth of a child creates immediate readiness for change and the willpower to see it through. For others, the process is a deliberate choice to make a change for the better. No matter what road brought you to this point, the first step in experiencing *The Shake Up* is to stand down – to pause and think before taking immediate action.

Our past experiences prepare us for what is to come and we use those experiences to make decisions about what is happening now. Consider how the experiences and interactions you had in the past have influenced your current behavior. After so many times of being hurt we tend to build defenses. We have had our hearts broken, been misled by colleagues at work, or gotten pranked by "friends." We go into survival mode and start developing a thick skin. Unfortunately, our thick skin often goes together with a closed mind. We get set in our ways and in our thoughts and start reflexively defending ourselves against everyone. We stop letting new concepts in and we begin to view everything through our cynical goggles. Stand down does not mean stop looking out for yourself; it means pause before you act and use compassion as a part of your action process. By standing down we prepare ourselves to listen and receive. We can quiet our knee-jerk reactions and allow for deeper thought and clearer action. By remembering to stand down you stop missing opportunities and begin making changes in your life.

Day 1

Fashion Critic

On an unseasonably warm October evening Alexis was getting out of her car to head into a restaurant to meet friends. As she was pulling her purse from the back seat a woman yelled, “You can’t wear white pants after Labor Day!” Stunned and confused, Alexis looked up just in time to see an older model SUV speeding away with its passenger quickly rolling up the window.

React with Kindness

Who does that?! At some point, we all have. We have come to a snap judgment based on our own hang-ups and let it fly without any regard for the person on the other end of our outburst. The pants fit Alexis well, no bulging or bunching, and they were paired with a simple black top. Even so, she became the victim of a drive-by criticism.

Before we speak, let's engage our brain to mouth filter. Think about whether the comment needs to be made. What's the purpose? Ask yourself, am I saying this to be hurtful, to make myself feel superior, or do I really need to say something? Have I examined the situation with compassion? In the case of Alexis, the yeller had no accountability. She raced away before Alexis could turn around, let alone respond.

We need to hold ourselves accountable for all of our statements, whether they are made to a person's face or behind their back. If you would not want the person to hear what you are saying, don't say it. If you are not comfortable making the comment directly to their face and receiving a response, the comment may not be necessary. If things are so out of hand you really need to say something, find a way to do it calmly and privately in a way which doesn't embarrass or demean the person.

Extend this concept beyond the words you say and allow it to take over the way you think. By training ourselves to pause before we speak, we can train ourselves to think in a more positive manner about those around us. Even without verbalizing those positive thoughts, they will have an effect on our actions.

I've always seen the good in people and been diplomatic about their faults. However, as I became increasingly stressed and more critical of my own life I began to lose my positive attitude. I was having a major lack attack and it began to impact my relationships, with even my closest friends. When I purposely reacted with kindness and refocused my energy on my time-honored ways of acceptance and caring, my life got better. I had removed a layer of stress and anguish simply by choosing to do so.

Shake-Up: Compliment Someone

Put the power of positive thinking into practice. Find someone and pay them a compliment. Better if it is someone you don't know. Better still if it is someone you initially had a negative reaction towards and have found a way to compliment them anyway. Try to observe their reaction. Then notice how you feel.

Day 2

Time Signature

Knowing that Scott was interested in buying a house, Candice invited him to a party hosted by Rob, a realtor she recently met. During the party she noticed Rob and Scott talking and thought it was good they had found each other since she hadn't gotten a chance to make an introduction. Toward the end of the evening, after Scott had left, Rob came over and started to give a full report on how the night was going. With a smug smile he explained how this "moron" named Scott had said the song playing was in six-four, how he told him it was actually in twelve-eight, and how he would know because he was in a band.

Candice nodded and smiled allowing Rob to enjoy his moment of perceived victory. She decided not to mention Scott was just finishing up his PhD in music theory, or that he was interested in buying a house. Instead, she made a mental note to text Scott later and apologize for Rob's rude behavior.

Relationships Matter

Ah! If Rob only knew. Whether they are client referrals or helpful suggestions when a hiring manager has a position to fill, every job depends on relationships. Why lose the chance to build a positive one just to be right? Especially considering he was the host, Rob could have said, "Oh, I thought this was in twelve-eight" in a kind way and possibly opened the door to a friendly discussion. He may have even gained a client. Instead he allowed his ego to get in the way and – without knowing it – lost a sale.

There is no grand prize for being right all the time and the world will not implode if you miss one or two opportunities to share your superior correctness with those around you. Instead of reacting immediately when a situation occurs, pause, think, and react with compassion. Take a couple of seconds to consider the other person's point of view. See if there is a way to change the situation for the good of all involved.

Sometimes it is difficult to engage the brain to mouth filter fast enough. You know you should stop, but you just can't hit the brakes in time and the words come crashing out. We've all been there. When we react instantly we often get it wrong. We have been diligently practicing all this time to defend ourselves, and we end up defending against the wrong things. We defend against the shy and the quiet. We defend against the weak. We defend against those looking for help. We like to think of ourselves as strong, so we defend against that which is not like us when, in reality, we are much better served by diversity.

Humans build communities because we need a network of others for survival. When an opportunity arises to build a relationship, learn to recognize it and make the most of the situation. When you have the opportunity to do something helpful or kind, do it. The relationships I built with others at various jobs were always what carried me through to the next one. My boss at the zoo recruited me to work in an afterschool program more than six months after she had moved on. My clients and even my competitors at the dance studio called to hire me after we closed because I always maintained a positive relationship with them. Through those relationships, I was able to start my coaching business and create the schedule I needed for my family to be happy. Foster positive relationships in all your endeavors; you never know when they will pay off.

Shake-Up: Send a Smile

A smile is a universal greeting of happiness. I love to smile at the most unfriendly looking people and watch their expression instantly transform. Once, I was trying to change lanes while driving and the car next to me insisted on matching my speed and refusing to let me over. When we were aligned, I glanced over at the driver who was giving me the most stern, angry, mad-dog look he possibly could. Instead of making the situation worse by getting angry right back, I smiled. His behavior instantly changed. He smiled, then started to flirt. I seized the opportunity, slowed down enough to change lanes behind his car, and safely made my exit. Give smiling a try and watch the reactions you get.

Day 3

Hard Feelings

Esme promised to call Brooke at 8:30 pm to discuss the upcoming reunion picnic they were planning. Brooke was so exhausted from working late it was all she could do to fling off her shoes before lying down, yet she stayed awake until 11:00 pm waiting for Esme's call. She finally gave up and went to sleep. The next morning Brooke saw Esme never called. She was frustrated over losing two hours of potential sleep when she was super tired. As the day wore on, Brooke got more and more annoyed. She began cursing Esme with every long blink, yawn, and head nod. A couple of days later Brooke arrived early to their weekly Saturday morning meet-up ready to let

Esme know just how she felt about being stood up. As soon as Esme walked over to the table she started apologizing to Brooke. She told her the story from the other night. Esme's son had gotten sick and threw up in his bed. Before they could stop her, their dog jumped up onto the bed, ran through the mess, and tracked it all over the room. Esme and her husband had to shampoo the carpet, bathe the kid, bathe the dog, and wash all the bedding. Then they took turns holding their son until finally ending up in the emergency room where they learned he had salmonella and was severely dehydrated. He was just released from the hospital Friday evening.

Presume the Best

When was the last time someone you know didn't answer your text or show up when they said they would? What was your first reaction? Did you "just know" they were doing it on purpose? Were you "so sick" of them standing you up? Don't ascribe intent that isn't there. Most of the time people do not intend to be mean or rude, life just happens. They fell asleep and didn't call. They lost their job and could not afford to send you a holiday gift. While shopping they genuinely forgot you can not eat poppy seed muffins. There is no benefit to holding the anger in until you see them. It does not help you and it does not help those around you. If you are upset with someone all day at work for losing your favorite stapler, aren't you more likely to say something unkind to a person in your way at the store, or to pick a fight when you get home? Similarly, if you get into an argument with your spouse before you leave for work, aren't you more likely to be harsh with your co-workers? I am.

Until you learn the real story, presume the best. Use the fact this person is your friend or family member and they care about you as evidence they probably did not slight you intentionally. Ask questions and learn what happened, then decide what to do about the situation. If your friend did not call because they got a last minute invite to a restaurant opening and decided to go without you, it is your responsibility to let them know how that makes you feel. When someone keeps repeating a pattern you don't like, say something. They probably don't even know they hurt your feelings, so approach the situation with compassion. Do not continue being upset and letting it eat at you. Find a way to address the issue within yourself or with them, and find a way to move forward.

Shake-Up: Flip It

Next time you start getting worked up about someone slighting you remember to flip it. Think about what they are doing and then consider what would need to happen to make you display the same behavior. For example, Esme promised to call Brook. When she didn't call, Brook could flip it and think, "What would stop me from calling Esme if the situation were reversed?" Maybe Brook wouldn't have called if she had to work late, if she ran into an old friend and got caught up talking, or if she got distracted by a last minute project and remembered to call too late in the day. Try to put yourself in the other person's shoes and consider what might be happening on their end, not just what has happened on your side.

Day 4

Monster Truck

Michael and Tracy were driving along Interstate 10 enjoying the day. They were cruising with the windows down and the music up when a very large truck zoomed up behind them, swerved to the side cutting off another driver, sped up, and then swerved in front of their car. The monster truck was lifted about two feet taller than a regular truck, had huge tires, was painted black with neon green flames, had multiple bumper stickers in the back window, a row of six round lights across the roof, and a large scrotum dangling from the tow hitch. Tracy stared in disbelief. Michael's only comment, "A person can say so much with their vehicle."

Check Your Message

Michael was right. You can speak volumes with your vehicle. The bumper stickers, the level of cleanliness, the items hanging from the rearview mirror… or the tow hitch. You may not have much choice about the vehicle you drive. You might drive the used one your parents bought when you were in high school, or the one your neighbor was selling because it was the only one you could afford. You might drive a van because you have five kids or because you must take your grandmother to physical therapy and you need room for her wheelchair. Even if you don't have control over what you drive, you have control over how you treat it and how you adorn it. Throw out the trash, run it through the car wash once in awhile, and think carefully before you start adding accessories.

Your vehicle is not the only thing which relays your message. This applies to your home, your work space, your clothing, your hair, your body modifications. You may have to make due with limited resources, but you have control over how you treat your possessions and yourself as well as how you put what you have together. Consider the message you are sending to others: approachable, helpful, kind, grouchy, standoffish, angry. Are you sending the message you want to send?

Your message may not be coming across only in your appearance. It can come across in your actions and in your words. Do you stand with your arms crossed or spend most of your time looking down at your phone instead of talking to those around you? Do you say you like all people and then tell racist jokes? Do you start sentences with, “I don’t want to be mean, but…”? If you do, the message you are sending might be pushing people away. Without realizing it you might be saying, “I am a jerk. I do not value myself or others. Quality people should not associate with me.” You could be preventing beneficial relationships.

I am not good at hiding my feelings from my face. If I am hurt, angry, or frustrated, it usually shows. I realized a while back that sometimes the message my face was sending was not the message I wanted to send. To fix this I intentionally made an effort to send the message I wanted to send with my face and body language. No matter how stressful things were, when one of my co-workers or staff came to my office door I smiled and welcomed them in. When I am exhausted and just want to sit on the couch and zone out I make an effort to listen to the stories my kids want to share about their day. I make an effort to understand what my husband is doing at his job. Even though I don't have the training to truly understand every bit of the code he is producing I can follow the concepts, learn the lingo, and keep track of what his new projects are for various clients. I want my message to be that I care – because I do. Sometimes I get wrapped up in my own projects and forget to let people know I care, so I make a conscious effort to send them a message of caring through my actions. By sending positive messages I enhance relationships. By being aware of the message you are sending you can create a closer connection with those around you.

Shake-Up: Edit

Find something you have, use, do, or say which you need to edit. It could be time to donate the weird shirt you have been wearing for 15 years or stop telling the really rude joke you like which no one else thinks is funny. Maybe you cut people off in the middle of their stories with one of your own, or you regularly post vague messages on social media. (e.g. Ugh, I'm so annoyed right now.) If you are not sure ask someone you trust to tell you the truth, and don't get upset with them when they do. Only choose one thing. Do not stress yourself out trying to make half a dozen edits at once. To complete this Shake-Up make one change. If you are inspired to make another one afterwards, go for it.

Day 5

Wednesday Morning

Amara stayed up half the night finishing an important presentation for work. She forgot to check her alarm before going to sleep and it went off 30 minutes early the next morning. Annoyed and disoriented she fell back to sleep almost immediately. By the time she woke up again she was running 20 minutes late. On the way to work she spilled coffee on her shirt, and when she arrived the office manager told her the presentation had been moved up from 2:00 pm to 11:00 am.

Focus Up

It is so easy to get caught up in worries and bogged down by daily tasks, we forget to find the fun. You might not like your job, but it does have the reward of a paycheck. Maybe it has other rewards you are missing because you have closed yourself off. Perhaps it offers time to listen to an audio book during your commute, or frequent a great restaurant where you have lunch on Fridays. Or maybe it's the cute delivery person who stops by twice a week. In Amara's case, she was thankful she chose to stay up and finish the presentation. She didn't have to scramble to finish it before the new meeting time. She found a sweater in her desk drawer which covered the coffee stain, and went into the meeting well prepared and in good spirits. By presenting earlier in the day – and nailing it – she got invited by the Regional Vice President to a long lunch on the company dime. They discussed her future within the company and a potential promotion.

Stop focusing down and spending your energy complaining about all the little things which don't go your way. Focus up, find the bright side, and start enjoying the positives in life. Purposely look for things you like and "live 'em up". When something goes well, even if it's a small thing, use the positive event to boost your mood and carry you through. When something comes along which is not your favorite, bear down, get through it as quickly as possible, then move on to something else.

It's ok to feel bad, mad, or sad and it is acceptable to express those feelings. There is no requirement to feel or act happy all the time. In my experience, fake happy tends to be more destructive than genuine unhappy. Make an effort to find the joy and don't let something trivial ruin your whole day. It is up to you to decide what's trivial just like it is up to you to focus up instead of down.

Shake-Up: List 5 Positives

Create a list of five (5) positive things which recently happened to you. Be sure to label the top of the list "Positives." It does not matter if the five things you write down are large or small; any five positive things will work. When the list is done save it where you can find it later. We'll come back to this list near the end of the book.

Part 2

Tune In

Now that you have quieted yourself by learning to stand down, it is time to tune in and start listening to the world around you. By tuning in I have been able to help friends before they knew they needed my help. Like when I dropped a friend off at the airport and she forgot to tell me when to pick her up. I knew what day she was supposed to return, so I kept my afternoon open. When she texted me in a panic the morning of her arrival I told her not to worry because I was available to pick her up when her flight landed. I have been able to solve problems before they got out of control, and I use trends I've noticed to help my life run more smoothly. After a few years (I didn't say I learned quickly!) I noticed when my daughter was sick to her stomach she would always throw up three times. I started insisting she stay near the facilities until the three times were over. This one observation has saved us a ton of sheet washing and carpet scrubbing. Tune in and take notice of what is going on around you. You can use this knowledge to the benefit of yourself and others.

Day 6

Parked

After a Justin Timberlake concert Cody and Amber were belted into her Toyota and waiting to get out of the parking structure along with four-thousand other people. During their wait they witnessed an interesting scene: A nearby car had gotten a flat tire right in the middle of the aisle. They were trying to use an automatic pump (some sort of deal that plugs into the cigarette lighter) to fill the tire and get moving. At one point they did get the car moving, but instead of pulling into the first open parking space to sort it out, they kept going in the line – predictably they got stuck again. This time they blocked a car trying to back out into traffic. The passenger in the car rolled down their window, leaned out, and started yelling for them to move. Helpful? Not so much. A woman driving a monstrous SUV started inching her way into a non-existent spot in the line. The line of cars was not moving at all, but a truck coming down a near-by ramp decided he might be able to help by honking.

Cody and Amber figured they weren't going anywhere for awhile so they rolled up the windows, put on a CD they purchased while exiting the concert, and talked about their favorite moments from the performance. Security cleared up the chaos in less than 15 minutes and they had a smooth drive home.

Watch & Wait

If the other drivers had taken a moment to assess the situation they may have noticed the flat tire. Someone might have been able to provide actual help. Pause and look around before reacting or overreacting. When you take time to observe the whole situation you gain a better perspective and can make a better decision. Cody and Amber acknowledged they would need to sit and wait a few minutes. They found a way to make the best of their situation. Letting go of their frustration about being delayed allowed them to enjoy the rest of their evening instead of ruining it.

Shake-Up: Chill

Once I stopped trying to rush everything I started feeling more relaxed. I drive the speed limit or less and let others go around. I use time waiting in line as my time to think, to dream, to plan, or to simply zone out. For this shake-up, wait in line patiently. Remember, the line giveith and the line takeith away. Sometimes you get through quickly and sometimes you get stuck behind the person who argues about the cost of a two dollar item, has 27 coupons, and wants to pay by writing a check. Forget about huffing and puffing, moaning and groaning, tapping and shifting. Just relax and wait. You will get there when you get there. Use the time waiting to tune in to yourself and your thoughts or to tune in to those around you.

Day 7

Spoiler Alert

Brian and Stephanie had Brian's parents over for dinner. In an attempt to make conversation, Brian's mom asked Stephanie if she had seen the new movie about some people trapped on an airplane. Stephanie said they had not seen it yet, but they were really looking forward to seeing it in the new luxury theater the following weekend. Brian's mother got all excited and began telling Stephanie the movie was about two main guys on a plane, one younger, and one older. Then she went into the back-story of the characters. Stephanie tried to stop her by mentioning they were planning to see the movie, but it did not matter. Brian's mom continued and insisted she wasn't giving anything away. Brian's dad cut in to say she might be telling too much and Brian tried to change the topic, but she just kept on. She missed all the social queues to stop; like when Stephanie got up to take dishes to the sink and when Brian suggested they may be more comfortable in the living room. After a 20 minute soliloquy about everything except the very last scene, Brian's mother had pretty much ruined any remaining suspense the movie might have held. All the way up to the bitter end she insisted she "wasn't really giving anything away."

Be Considerate

Once, similar events happened to me about five times within three weeks. When this happens the frustration isn't finding out what happens in the story; it is someone's failure to take your feelings or requests into consideration when telling their story. A spoiler feels like a mini-betrayal. The other person was so involved in sharing their own experience they failed to consider yours. Positive relationships are built on mutual trust. To create a relationship which is beneficial to both parties, each person must tune in to what the other person needs and wants. Sometimes you need to be willing to listen more than talk.

Shake-Up: Listen

Get some practice in listening and observing. You can listen to the birds, to nearby conversations, to nature, to traffic, or anything happening around you. Spend at least 10 minutes focusing on what you might usually ignore, and try to pick up on something new. Sometimes when my brain is distracted by focusing on the outside world I can subconsciously solve problems I couldn't previously solve while focusing directly on them. Sometimes when I listen and observe I hear familiar sounds such as a train in the distance. Other times I hear something interesting like a parent explaining to a child why the leaves change color in the fall. What do you observe when you listen?

Day 8

Empty Plate

Freddie had been working for a large corporation as a client account manager for almost two years. He was good at his job and a fairly nice guy, but his co-workers didn't know him very well. He usually ate at his desk or met his girlfriend for lunch rather than eating with others in the office. Most of the time he skipped the company happy hours, picnics, and holiday parties, and he wasn't particularly interested in what was happening in his co-workers' lives. Freddie figured work was for working and all the other stuff was not very important. Unfortunately, Freddie did not pay attention to what was happening within the company either. He failed to notice he was not being assigned any new clients. Not even when one of his client accounts left or failed to renew when their contract ended. In fact, he was starting to enjoy the lighter workload and felt like things must be going really well.

When his boss was promoted within the company and transferred to another state, a new manager was promoted from within the department. Freddie wasn't considered for the position. Several months later when the company went through a round of layoffs he was one of the first to be let go. Freddie's new manager had worked with him since he started in the department, but she did not really know him. His client accounts had been dwindling and there was no other information for her to use in her evaluations.

Zone In

Poor Freddie was totally zoned out when it came to his work environment. He did not notice changes in the company and he did not make an effort to interact with those around him. Had he made friends with his co-workers or spent a few lunches in the break room he might have learned about the state of the company and been able to request new clients – or worked harder to keep the ones he had. He could have shown initiative by offering to take on other projects or help those in the department who were overwhelmed. If he had interacted with the people around him the new manager may have been less willing to let him go.

Whether it is at work, at school, or at home we can easily get into the mode of just phoning it in. To succeed in our relationships, we need to change to zoning in. Watching changes in people's behavior and attitude has helped me know when to offer congratulations and when to offer sympathy. It helps me determine when to pass them a tissue and when to bust out the snacks I usually keep in my bag. In turn, when I have needed a hand, people have almost always been willing to help. So, visit with the weird guy at the copy machine and learn the name of your cube-mate's second child. Sure, it may not seem important now, but when one of them transfers to the new building and is asked to recommend someone to fill a vacancy they might remember how attentive you were and recommend you for the promotion. Zone in on the details of what is happening around you so you can avoid missing the subtle cues, like Freddie.

Shake-Up: Bring Snacks

Surprise people at your office (or another group you belong to) with snacks or something else they would appreciate. Whatever you bring does not need to be big. The idea is not to show off but to do something nice. Consistent, small gestures are much more genuine than large sweeping ones. Try to find ways to build and solidify relationships with those around you by sharing kindness.

Day 9

Type Type

Marisol was curled-up on the couch, snuggled in her pajamas and a blanket, typing intently on her laptop when her roommate Kris walked in.

Marisol: *type type type type*

Kris: How's it going?

Marisol: Fine. *type type type type*

Kris: How was your day?

Marisol: Good. *type type type type*

Kris: Do you want to watch a movie?

Marisol (as politely as possible): No thanks. *type type type*

Kris: What are you doing?

Marisol: Writing. *type type*

Kris: Oh… I saw Jon and Karen at the coffee shop today. They were having a huge fight!

Marisol: Hum, I hope they work it out. *type*

Kris: I don't know if they will. He seemed pretty mad and she started crying. She was trying to hide it, but I could tell. Oh! And then Liam walked in, but wouldn't make eye contact with anyone…

Marisol: *smiles, closes laptop, and turns her attention toward Kris*

Crack the Code

People speak in code all the time. Part of tuning in and being compassionate is learning how to pick up on their cues. If someone is not making eye contact or if all the answers to your questions are super short then they probably don't want to talk to you right now. Not necessarily because they don't like you, they might just be busy, or shy, or thinking, or tired. Try to notice what is going on with others from their perspective, not just yours. Even though Kris had blinders on, Marisol realized Kris really, really wanted to tell a story. Recognizing the importance of the story to her friend, Marisol took a break from her writing and listened.

Friends can be the ones who help you get through the toughest times. They rescue you from difficult situations and they help you laugh away the pain. They listen to all your crazy stories and sympathize when times are hard. Tune in to when they need you, even if their needs get in the way of what you are doing at the time. By helping my friends, I now have people in my life who will come over at ten o'clock at night and help change the battery in a chirping smoke detector 20 feet up on the ceiling. Friends who have given me their alarm code to get into their house if I need to borrow a humidifier while they are at work.

Avoid taking your friends for granted. Listen when they need to talk and show up when they need help. Give when you can because you will need to be on the receiving end one day.

Shake-Up: Friend Focus

Do something nice for a friend, show them how much you value them. Surprise them by picking up their favorite coffee or smoothie on the way to their house. Offer to watch their children while they go out with their spouse or to pay for a sitter so you can go out together. Surprise them by washing their car or mowing their lawn (if they won't read too much into it and get offended). Choose anything you know they would like or just spend time having fun together. Try to stay out of trouble and don't combine it with a birthday gift or an event you already have planned. If they ask why you are being so nice simply tell them it's because you like them.

Day 10

Ice Cream Sunday

When I was about 12 my family went out for ice cream. It was a hot day, so my ice cream was melting quickly and I kept getting chocolate ice cream on my face. All three of them were pointing it out and telling me where to wipe next. I was cleaning my face almost as much as I was eating the ice cream; I got frustrated. I asked them to stop telling me where the mess was until I was done. Well, they stopped alright. When we got home I saw I had been walking around for the past three hours with chocolate ice cream all over my chin and cheek. How embarrassing – especially at that age! Feeling hurt I asked my mom why they didn't tell me. She responded they tried to, but I told them to stop, so they stopped.

Listen Up

What I meant was they should stop until I was finished. Without realizing it I spoke with tween girl attitude and they stopped altogether. Even though they allowed me to look like a toddler all afternoon, they stood by me. We walked in and out of stores with my face covered in dried ice cream and they never pretended they didn't know me or that I wasn't part of the group. It was my overreaction and huffy attitude which prevented me from hearing their advice and accepting their help.

Our families, biological or otherwise, can help us more than we realize. They help us edit and filter and they often offer advice and suggestions which could save us time, effort, and grief if only we would listen up. When we ignore the recommendations given by those who love us we risk making fools of ourselves. Tune in to those who have your best interest at heart and keep an open mind when someone who truly cares about you tries to give you advice. You may end up going your own way, but at least take the time to consider wearing a different hat today or not getting that lower back tattoo.

Shake-Up: List 5 Relationships

Create a list of five (5) people or relationships which help or empower you. These might be people who comfort you, advise you, or listen to you. They are the people you care about the most, and the ones who care about you. Make sure this list is labeled "Relationships" and save it with your "Positives" list where you can find it later.

Part 3

Let Go

We can be our own worst enemy. We hang on to that which hurts us, ignore our own internal signals, and hold ourselves back, often out of fear. In college I took up ballroom dancing and I was pretty good. After graduation, life happened, and I stopped dancing for 10 years. When I finally went back I was recovering from a knee injury, wasn't sure how many patterns I remembered, and I was in a new town where I didn't know anyone. It was super hard to attend those first few Friday night practice dances. I was nervous about not remembering what I was doing, and I've always been naturally shy. I really wanted to dance, but no one asked me because they were accustomed to dancing with people they already knew. After about a month I realized if I was going to dance, I had better start getting to know some people. I let go of all the junk in my head and started asking guys to dance. Surprise, surprise, they were all very nice and they all said, "Yes." Eventually, I made friends and the regular dancers got to know me.

Sometimes, I still get nervous about asking people to dance. Occasionally, they do say, "No." And that's ok. I really love dancing and I have learned all the fun I experience by letting go of my fears far outweighs the anxiety laden half-comfort I feel when hiding in my own little space. Whether it is internal or external, let go of what is holding you back and do what you know is right for you.

Day 11

Team Vortex

Sandra and Elwyn were talking over pizza one night and came up with a really great idea for an app. They agreed to start working on it the next week. When they got together Sandra wanted to look at other apps to see how they functioned. She wanted to design some practice apps before they got started on their actual app. Elwyn wanted to get coding right away, but he went along with Sandra's suggestions. At their second meeting Elwyn had mapped out some of the app, but Sandra didn't have time to work on the user interface before the meeting as they had agreed. Sandra kept shifting the conversation. They spent most of the meeting discussing what they should do for marketing, possible pun-filled names, and schedules for rolling out updates after the app was released. Months went by and several meetings were canceled by Sandra. After a couple more non-productive meetings, Elwyn gave up on Sandra and started designing the app himself. Two weeks later, an app which did exactly what they had planned hit the market and became a huge success.

Go Now

If people are holding you back you have three choices: let them, bring them with you, or leave them behind. You know what you need to do to move forward. Whether you like it or not, you know. Sometimes it is a hard reality to face. Watch for those who are willing to help you and will make the process easier. When they come along, go. When you receive a sign, go. When you feel you want to, go. Do not wait for the perfect moment or the best possible time. It will never come. Go Now. Don't third, fourth, and fifth guess yourself – Go Now. You may stumble; you may not go far today, but that doesn't matter. Go Now.

Shake-Up: Dance

Shut the door, turn on some music, and dance for at least 10 minutes. Get your heart rate up and those endorphins flowing. Whenever I don't feel like doing anything is the time when I know I need to do something. Dancing is more fun than plain old exercising and it really can make you feel ready to conquer the world.

Day 12

Mama's Boy

Ivan and Sabrina had been dating for almost two years, and were getting pretty serious. While Sabrina was technically still living with her parents, she spent most of her time with Ivan at his parents' house. She was finishing school and they were saving money to get a place together.

Ivan's mother was upset Sabrina was not paying rent or doing any chores around the house. Sabrina said she used her car to drive family members to the grocery store and doctor's appointments and never asked for gas money. She pointed out she was either at school or at work most of the time and only at their house an hour or two in the evenings to eat and socialize with the family before bedtime.

Ivan tried to look busy in a corner. He didn't defend Sabrina at all, and when his mother asked what he thought he said maybe Sabrina should do some of the cleaning to help out if she did not want to pay rent. Sabrina broke up with Ivan in less than a week.

Break Away

Sabrina realized she was not the top priority in Ivan's life and he was not mature enough to defend her as his partner. Rather than shy away from the discussion, Ivan should have taken the opportunity to engage his mother about why she suddenly wanted Sabrina to pay rent when she never mentioned it in the previous six months. There may have been a possible solution. Perhaps Ivan could do more chores since he was not in school and only working part time, or Ivan and Sabrina could move out sooner than they had planned. Like

Sabrina, surround yourself with those who empower you and let go of those who do not have your back.

Shake-Up: Clean House

When I get overwhelmed or frustrated I have what I call a "cleaning fit." I scrub, vacuum, clean, and organize until I start feeling better. I feel the best when I get stuff I no longer need out of the house. Choose three items you do not need or are not using and throw them away, give them away, or donate them to charity. Experience the refreshing lightness of not being bogged down by that which no longer benefits you.

Day 13

Check Please

Emily's mother and stepfather were visiting from out of town for the weekend. Near the end of dinner at a local restaurant, wherein Emily's stepfather, Donald, had harassed the waitress within an inch of her sanity, the check arrived. When Emily's husband Henry offered to pay, Donald said, "Hang on." and took the check holder. He looked at the bill, mulled it over, and then handed it back to Henry saying, "Well, ok, you can pay."

Have Some Give

Most of us know this is rude, but apparently not all of us do. Emily and Henry have three children, so a bill for seven at a restaurant was not going to be small. Was Donald checking to see if it was too expensive for Henry to handle? This would be the best possible scenario. If after looking at the bill Donald determined the full amount was more than he was willing or able to cover, he could have offered to pay for his portion.

As a testament to his graciousness, Henry paid for the entire meal and as they were leaving pretended to have forgotten something. He went back, found the waitress, gave her an extra $20 tip, and apologized for Donald's behavior.

Giving is not just about giving money. Giving is also about learning to have flexibility – to yield a little. Confronting Donald would have caused tension in the family. Knowing they lived over 1,600 miles away and were only visiting for the weekend, Henry did what he thought was right without putting his wife in the uncomfortable position of playing referee. Let the frustration fall away and have compassion for those who don't have a clue they have been rude or insensitive.

Shake-Up: Relax

Start by relaxing your body from the top down. Neck rolls, shoulder rolls, leaning to each side, deep breathing, and so on. Shake out the knots and frustration while focusing on feeling more calm and open. The next time you are given the opportunity to be gracious stretch yourself and seize the moment. Forgive without being asked. Have some give and solve a difficult situation with compassion instead of conflict.

Day 14

Smooth Move

Justin and Kendra were married for just over four years when they had their first child. They both worked while Kendra's mother watched the baby during the day. They didn't make much money, but they were making ends meet and staying out of debt. After the birth of their second child things got more tiring and stressful, but Kendra was determined to make their marriage a success. She went to work early so she could get home in time to cook dinner for their family. She enlisted her friends to watch the kids over the weekend so they could have time alone together, but it did not seem to help. Justin became more and more distant: always watching TV, working on projects in the garage, or going out with friends. Soon however, she thought things were getting better. He started asking how her day was and he even brought her flowers once. A few weeks later a friend called to tell her she had seen Justin having an intimate dinner with another woman.

At first, Kendra was devastated but hey, it was just dinner. Maybe there was an innocent explanation. That night she confronted Justin. He confessed to having an affair, saying things like, "Well, it just sort of happened" and "She just kept asking me to date her."

Distraught, Kendra filed for divorce. She gained primary custody of the children and now had to work even harder as a single mother. Justin failed to make the assigned child support payments, claiming he couldn't afford them. Eight months after their divorce Kendra was on Facebook and saw photos of Justin with his girlfriend on vacation in Cancun

– at the exact same resort where they went for their honeymoon.

Forgive for Yourself

Well, that burns. Forget salt in the wound. This is like chopping jalapeños without gloves, forgetting to wash your hands, and then rubbing your eyes. A betrayal like this is hard to recover from. You just want to hide from the world doing whatever repetitive behavior you find most comforting: eating, sleeping, shopping, watching TV, something more destructive. You know what your favorites are. After your time of self pity, try to remember there are people in the world who need you. You need you! Don't let the jerk ruin your life – it's *your* life.

Forgiveness is not for them it is for you. Nothing can hold you back like the unwillingness to forgive. The pain consumes your thoughts, colors your feelings, and influences your actions. Just like planting a garden or raising a child, the things you nurture are the ones that thrive. If you nurture your frustration and anger they will grow into hate, and that is all you will have. Actual forgiveness is a process, and it takes time. It may even take professional counseling – and that's ok. To begin, focus on being willing to forgive. Allow yourself to want to let go of the anger and the pain. Then you can figure out what steps you will need to take to truly forgive.

Forgiveness gives you control over your feelings and your thoughts. It takes time to forgive someone for what they have done. Remember, holding hate in your heart eats away at your soul, so be patient and do not give up on reclaiming your life.

Shake-Up: Look Up

No need to panic. I'm not going to ask you to forgive some big injustice in one day. That would be unrealistic and unreasonable. Instead, do something you may not have done since you were a little kid – lie down under a tree. This is one of my favorite exercises and I don't do it often enough. For at least 10 minutes be still and look up into the branches. Collect your thoughts or let them run free. Listen up, observe, relax, think, let go.

Day 15

Cheerleader

One evening our friends took us to a local hockey game. It was fun even though our team wasn't doing very well. We all clapped and cheered for awhile, but after about an hour most of us got tired and focused more on our nachos than cheering. My younger daughter kept right on cheering even when our team missed. My older daughter – who was easily embarrassed at that age – tried to get her to sit down, but my youngest wasn't having it. At the end of the game a couple from a few rows over came up and handed her the puck they had caught at the beginning of the game. They congratulated her on all her cheering and told her how wonderful it was she had such a positive spirit.

Never Mind

It's not always others who are holding you back. Much of the time it is you. You are in your own head stopping yourself from getting where you need to go. Mind has two meanings: a person's intellect and a person's attention. Stop over-thinking and stop giving your attention to what others might be thinking. Instead, choose to never mind.

Never mind trying to save face. Never mind the crowd around you. Never mind what critics will say. Wear what you like, eat what you need, do activities you want to do. Choose to stop worrying about whether or not everyone is watching or approves and follow your heart. (Uh, by the way, if your heart says become a cat burglar, serial killer, or some other nefarious thing, seek professional help.)

Some people can begin living their truth in one fell swoop. They cut ties with those who are disrupting their peace and begin following their own path. Not all of us are so bold. We over think, we ponder, we consider, we make excuses, we are shy, but if we choose to, we can change.

Shake-Up: List 5 Never Minds

You don't have to make changes instantly or accomplish all your goals in one afternoon. You can make small changes over time and by doing so slowly, steadily, reach happiness.

Create a list of five things you want to never mind again. Maybe you keep worrying about what your neighbors think of your car. Perhaps you are staying up nights thinking about what people are really saying about your new haircut. You could be stressed out because you accidentally hit "Reply All" on that email at work today, or because it's fund drive season. Everyone you know is about to ask you to buy something you don't really want from their kid's school and you have no spare cash. What do you want to stop wasting your brain power on? I'm almost always cold. People continuously harass me for wearing jackets in the summer and extra layers in the winter. For a number of years I tried to "tough it out" and be silently cold. No longer! I stopped letting their comments bother me and now I wear a jacket (or three) whenever I feel cold, and I never mind what people think or say about it.

A never mind could also be something you want to remove from your life so you can stop thinking about it, perhaps 10 pounds, an excessive collection of shoes, or a detrimental habit like smoking. Whatever it is that you want to let go, put it on your list of "Never Minds" and save it. We'll go back to it on Day 30. By the way, you've just finished Day 15. You're half way there!

Part 4

Look Inside

The best you have to offer is within you. Somehow we tend to forget that. We get down on ourselves for not being perfect. We put up walls to keep people out. We stop considering advice and refuse to accept compliments. We try to present what we think is the perfect image. It's time to take a good look inside and figure out who is really in there. Start owning up to the real you and listening to it. Be truthful about who that person is with yourself and with others. For a short time I tried to be one of those people who likes to go out and party. While I do love social dancing, I rarely enjoy super-loud thumpy music, excessive drinking, or staying up past midnight. I just can't hang. After trying this lifestyle multiple times because I wanted to fit in, I gave up on being someone I wasn't and stopped going to these types of events unless I really wanted to go. I am so much happier! When you admit the truth about who you are you can weed through all the noise, focus on your best qualities, and start using them to your advantage.

Day 16

Honey Do

Brittany asked her husband, Drew, to clean the garage. He said that he would, but he kept putting it off with a new excuse: too hot, too windy, kids need a ride to soccer practice, have to go to the grocery store, anything. The longer he took, the more she pressed. The more she asked about it, the more annoyed he got, and the more he resisted getting it done.

Own Up

Unknown to his wife, Drew had an almost crippling fear of spiders. He would have rather set the garage on fire with his Magpul Ronin 1125R motorcycle inside than have a surprise run-in with a spider. Having been teased in the past, Drew was really embarrassed about his fear and did not want to appear weak.

Had Drew told Brittany his feelings when she first asked him to clean out the garage they might have been able to work out another arrangement. They could clean the garage together or she could clean the garage while he did a different chore. If they were both afraid of spiders they might be able to hire someone to help fumigate and clean. Perhaps a move to Antarctica would have solved the problem? I hear the hot springs are nice. More seriously though, instead of building up animosity for several weeks, a few honest words from Drew and a bit of compassion from Brittany could have led to a simple and equitable solution.

Shake-Up: Practice Honesty

Before you start this Shake-Up I want to mention what honesty is not. Honesty is not a weapon to be used to hurt others or veil your slights against them. Too often I observe people using the word honesty to describe what is actually cruelty. If someone asks, "How do you like my new sweater?" and you respond with, "That sweater is super ugly. I hate that color. Sorry, just being honest!" you are using honesty as a license to be cruel. Instead, respond truthfully in a kind and compassionate way. For example, "It's not my favorite color, but it fits you well."

Now, for this Shake-Up we're practicing honesty. The next time you are confronted with a question or situation, answer honestly even if it feels difficult to do so. I first started practicing this at potlucks. Ever go to a potluck where one person is just raving about their own dish and trying to force everyone to eat it? If you don't want to offend them and say you like it when you really do not, they will remember. Then they will make that thing and expect you to eat it at every single potluck until the end of time. I found it is so much better to be kind, compassionate, and honest right from the beginning.

Day 17

One Up

Kevin was absentmindedly twisting his wedding ring while leaning against the counter in his parent's galley kitchen and watching a delivery team maneuver his father's new TV through the front door. His mother was guarding her potted plants and ceramic elephant collection, while his father was directing the pair of movers to just the right spot. To make it seem as if he was busy doing something other than staring, Kevin was putting away one or two clean dishes every few minutes. When they finished opening the box and putting it on the stand the 70" TV absolutely dominated the cozy 12' x 15' living room and blocked a third of the doorway to the bedroom.

Kevin figured he would have to turn his head to see the whole screen, and watching anything while sitting on the couch was going to feel like being stuck in the front row at a movie theater.

Kevin's father excitedly relayed the story of how he had gotten such a good deal on such a large TV. Then, he insisted on hooking everything up and playing something so everyone could see how great the new TV was. Kevin couldn't help thinking about his own new TV. It was smaller, 46", and worked perfectly for the space in his living room. He remembered how his father was looking at it a few weeks before; asking where he purchased it and how much it had cost. He realized tonight's dinner invitation had been staged to make sure Kevin was on-site for the big delivery. It reminded him of when he bought his new phone, and when his wife gave him a watch for their anniversary. Each time his father had shown up a few weeks later with something bigger and flashier.

Be True

Don't be Kevin's dad. Focus on your own goals, what you want to achieve, and how you can better yourself. A little competition can be motivating, but when you are competing against the people you should be helping like your family, competition can become harmful. Kevin's dad was so focused on out shining Kevin he forgot to assess what he actually wanted and needed. Instead, he kept trying to one-up those around him and was never truly satisfied. Instead of comparing yourself to others simply compare you now to you in the past. If you've made progress, you're good. If you haven't, turn it around.

Be true to yourself. Do activities you like, not just the ones everyone else is doing. Work towards your own goals even if they are not the most interesting or exciting to others. If they excite and inspire you, they are worthwhile. Avoid trying to force yourself to use certain vocabulary or act in a way which is completely opposite of your true personality simply because you are keeping up with the latest trend or think it will make you fit in with the crowd. I no longer have any shame about not wanting to ride the craziest roller coasters. I was pressured onto one which looked beyond my tolerance once and was miserable for the entire 1 minute, 45 seconds of it. Never again!

As a side note: Politeness and good manners are not simply a trend (although they do seem to fall in and out of fashion). Politeness and good manners are beneficial because they help us function together as a society. Being true to yourself is not a free pass to start being rude to everyone else. It is an invitation to stop being rude to yourself and to stop forcing yourself to do things with the sole intention of fitting in or standing out.

Shake-Up: Do You

Find something which is totally you and do it. Maybe it is a project you started and haven't gotten to finish. Maybe it is taking a class you cannot convince any of your friends to take with you. Go do something uniquely you. You might play music, organize your closet, go for a run, or cook your favorite meal. I'll probably be out dancing.

Day 18

Humble Pie

Roommates Derek and Ethan were part of the Banquets & Catering Services team at a local resort. A large convention was taking place, and hundreds of individual sized pies had been made for the farewell dinner. Derek wanted some of those pies. Ethan was mildly against it. Not enough to stand up for his ideals and say, "No," just enough to not steal the pies himself. After a lengthy discussion, it was agreed that Derek would take a few pies and Ethan would drive the car and pick him up in back of the kitchen.

When Ethan pulled around to pick him up, Derek was struggling to open the door while balancing three large boxes filled with pies. "Help!" Derek whispered. Not knowing what else to do, and worried they were about to get caught, Ethan got out of the car, opened the back door, and helped load the boxes. He drove home in a stunned silence while Derek laughed and smiled all the way. When they arrived Derek invited some friends over and they all laughed and ate. Ethan tried to join in the fun, but the more he ate the sicker he felt and eventually he went off to bed.

The next day at work, Derek was confronted about the theft. He had been recorded by the hidden security cameras in the kitchen and he was fired. Ethan was questioned, as was everyone who was working the same shift as Derek, but his participation was not discovered. Every time Ethan went to work he felt guilty about stealing, about lying, and about not stopping his roommate from making such a big mistake.

Gut Check

We all have an internal compass which tells us exactly what we should and should not do. Most of us listen some of the time, but have gotten very good at overriding the message when it doesn't suit us. When I was about seven months pregnant with my second child I had an idea for a small business. I invited two people I had previously worked with to be a part of the business with me. They sounded excited, and we all agreed to meet at a restaurant for dinner. They both stood me up. I'm stubborn, so I ate anyway and tried to pass off their not showing up as having simply forgotten. While driving home, nerves and pregnancy belly got the best of me and I threw up in my lap. I drove the rest of the way home all gross and crying. It was awful, but I did not tell anyone what had happened. When I spoke with each person later they both apologized for not showing up and said they did not think they had time to be a part of the company. Even though I knew in my gut them not showing meant my plan was not strong enough, I started the company anyway. I failed to listen to the overwhelming message my body was sending. Instead, I ignored my gut feeling, started the company, and spent hundreds of hours and thousands of dollars for very little return.

When you know something is not right, listen to the messages you are sending to yourself. Stop overriding the sick feeling in your stomach when it is trying to send you a warning. For example, if you are thinking of going on a date with your roommate's ex and you have a gut feeling they might be mad, pay attention to the feeling. Don't ignore your instincts because "the ex is really hot and they asked you, so it should be cool... right?" Listen to your gut when it tells you something is wrong, or prepare to face the consequences of poor choices and live with the feeling of regret.

Shake-Up: Go Out

Go out on your own. To dinner, to the movies, for coffee, anywhere you want. Be alone, but not lonely. Enjoy taking time to listen to yourself and do what you want to do. Focus on the internal messages you are sending. Start building the confidence to listen to yourself and the confidence to act on what your gut is telling you.

Day 19

Deal Breakers

Before Sarah married her second husband she sat him down at the little kitchen table in her tiny apartment for a talk. She told him she loved him very much and she wanted to marry him but, she had two conditions. For the first condition she said, "I am fat. I will always be fat. Do not expect this to change, and never ask me to lose weight." He agreed, and she went on to the second condition saying, "Never, ever leave me. I am committing to you for life and I expect you to do the same." He agreed to the second condition as well and they have been happily married for over 25 years.

Admit Truth

In her first condition Sarah admitted the truth about her weight and embraced her true self. She knew she could not and would not spend her life trying to change her body to suit someone else's expectations or requirements. She would have been unhappy if she had.

To better understand Sarah's second condition, you should know her first husband packed up and left only a few months after their baby was born. The pain of being abandoned by the person she expected to have as a life partner right after having his child almost destroyed her. Sarah knew she could never experience something like that again and remain sane. She admitted this truth to herself and to her fiancé. While harsh, for her it was necessary her partner understand how seriously she viewed their commitment and he value it just as much.

Once you admit who you are and what you need you can build towards happiness and peace. If you continue to keep your truth hidden instead of letting it show you will continue to be unsettled. Your character traits are part of you. Embrace them. All of them. Stop trying to ignore the parts which do not fit within a predetermined set of rules or expectations. Instead, be honest with yourself about who you really are – issues and all. Once you have honestly identified your traits it is time to admit them. Allow them to become part of your identity. When you accept all your traits you can begin to figure out how to use your assets and work through your weaknesses to reach your full potential.

I spent years trying to suppress my nurturing traits so I would appear more calm and casual. All the while the real me constantly wanted to check on people to see if they were okay. This is how I naturally am. I fix someone's shirt tag if it is sticking out and I tell them if they have a booger on their face.

I worry about my friends leaving the house without a jacket. After years of pretending to be cool and detached (with little success) I finally admitted I care. I want people to be happy and fulfilled. I want them to be comfortable and secure. After accepting my true nature, I realized my calling was to share this compassion with others and I turned it into my career. Listen to yourself. Admit truth. Have compassion for yourself and unlock your own happiness and peace.

Shake-Up: Take a Nap

Sleep provides renewal like nothing else. Drift off and let your unconscious get to work on solving issues for you. When I am tired I become overwhelmed so much more easily than when I'm rested. A nap is a chance to reset and rebuild both mental and physical strength. Even a nap after which I wake up confused about what day we're on, is better than not taking a nap. Once recovered, I feel rewarded for taking time to care for myself. If you can not fit a nap into the middle of your day, do not give up! Go to bed early one night or sleep in one morning. If you can't sleep just lay still, relax, and drift. Get the benefits of resting and allow the rested you to be more forgiving and accepting of the whole you.

Day 20

Reflection

Cameron wore the one suit he owned to every job interview until he finally got hired. Once hired, he realized he had better go out and buy some appropriate work wear before his first day. His girlfriend went with him and helped search for suits, shirts, ties, and sweaters. When something didn't work she would politely tell him, and he would take it off and put it in the "no" pile. When an outfit looked good she would compliment him, but he would find a problem. If she said the shirt was a nice color he would say it wasn't right for his skin tone. If she complimented the cut of the pants, he complained about his waistline being too big to make them hang properly.

Then he would go back to the dressing room. Every time he got back there he would stand in front of the mirror searching for flaws in how this great looking suit fit him. After several hours of searching for the best colors and sizes and trying on clothes, Cameron started to question if he was even qualified for the new job he was about to start.

Except Nothing

Cameron became so caught up in searching for flaws he started to doubt everything about himself. He had someone who cared for him enough to help with shopping sitting there giving him complements, yet he refused to internalize any of them. Do you reject compliments out of hand? Do you ever hear yourself saying or thinking things like the following?

I could be attractive except for my nose.

I am smart except I can't figure out how to fold a fitted sheet.

I might be good at dancing except I have two left feet.

I'm brave except I am afraid of heights.

What's the deal with all the exceptions? Have some compassion towards yourself! One exception does not negate an entire positive quality about you. Break these apart and think of them separately. Turn them into statements instead of exceptions.

I am attractive.

I have a unique nose.

I am smart.

I do not like folding fitted sheets.

I might be good at dancing.

I am shy.

I am brave.

I do not like heights.

When someone gives you positive feedback try to accept it. There are good things about you. I have been a performer for years and have learned the only way to have a good performance is to practice often and practice well. When the dress rehearsal is over and there is no time to think of what to do, we do what we have practiced. Practice focusing on the good you have to offer so you can build inner resilience and increase your happiness. Take "except" out of the equation and except nothing. Instead, accept the things you can not change and move forward. Accept it all. The good, the bad, the flawed, and the perfect. It's all yours: No exceptions.

Shake-Up: List 5 Qualities

Create a list of your five (5) best qualities or five (5) positive things about yourself. If you have trouble getting to five keep trying. You have way more than five positive qualities and you can find them if you allow yourself to look. If you really need help, ask a friend. Write your list, label it, and save it with your other lists until you reach Day 30. Hey, maybe you can add dedicated to your list! After all, you have made it through Day 20 and there are only 10 left to go.

Part 5

Do Better

Do better doesn't mean you are not already doing well. Do better means keep making continuous improvement. You have value and you have power. The choices you make have an impact on those around you. It is up to you to decide what kind of impact you want to make; a negative one or a positive one. When faced with such a choice step it up and do better. Be a leader, take chances, try new things. Use your qualities to the advantage of everyone. Discipline yourself to make better choices and to make a greater effort not because someone told you to, but because you want to, and you know you are capable. Begin to expect more from yourself. More patience, more kindness, more compassion for yourself and for others. More commitment, more focus, and fewer excuses. You know you can do better so go ahead and start.

Day 21

All Talk

The powers that be hired a new boss for the department where Dominic worked. The new department head seemed nice enough when everyone met her. She definitely knew how to say all the right things. During her first week, she set up a rigorous meeting schedule for the department. Staff was required to attend three meetings each week wherein they spent two hours per meeting developing a vision statement and a mission statement; identifying target service areas and their target audience; plus, creating lists of values, goals, and objectives for the department.

She also required everyone to create a list of their current projects. Then she assigned due dates to "increase productivity." Upper management wanted to cut down on overtime, so she informed the staff they would no longer be allowed to stay late. Dominic did his best to complete his projects on time. Being a well organized and conscientious person, he went to speak to the new boss well before one was due because he could see he was not going to finish it by the deadline. He asked to be allowed to attend fewer meetings until the project was complete. Nope. He asked if he could stay late like he used to do. No, must leave when work ends. Don't take work home with you. No paid overtime. He asked for a two week extension knowing that's how long he really needed to finish without modifying the rest of his schedule. Instead, she gave him a two day extension from Wednesday to Friday. Frustrated, he took it and did his best to finish, but could not. When he didn't make the deadline she formally reprimanded him and put a note in his file. Dominic started looking for a new job that night. He found one within a month and quit. Within six months everyone who had worked in the department before the new manager's arrival had transferred, retired, or quit.

Lead by Example

Dominic was a hard working employee before his new boss arrived on the scene. She did not take time to get to know her new staff, to find out how things were going, or to observe how the department functioned. She did not have much actual management experience, but she wanted to appear strong and capable; so she started off doing all of the things she *thought* a manager should do. In reality a leader should be working as hard or harder than anyone else in the group. They should give credit to their team when it is due, take the blame for failures, and listen to their people when they speak. A leader does not necessarily have to act on everything their staff says; however, even the most dedicated people in a team will lose heart if their leader never listens. The leader may be the team captain, but should still be part of the team.

Leadership is done by example and we should all behave like quality leaders. Do what you say you are going to do. Complete what you start. Hold yourself to a higher standard – one worthy of being followed.

Shake-Up: Finish Something

Whatever you have been putting off, get it done. It does not matter if it is a project, something that needs fixing, sending "thank you" cards, calling an old friend, or taking out the trash. Stop hiding under a pile of excuses and get it done.

Day 22

Nice Tie

When his father was diagnosed with cancer Brett left a job in pharmaceutical sales and moved back home to help his mother. Soon afterward, the economy declined. Brett took a job working on commission as a salesman at a furniture store to make ends meet. One afternoon a woman came in and told him, in a very rude way, his tie was ugly. Brett immediately wanted to say something snarky and biting, but he suspected she was only being mean to rattle his sales game; to prevent him or any other sales person from speaking to her and trying to make a sale. Instead of following his first instinct Brett collected himself, smoothed his tie, and said with a genuine, charismatic smile, "Yes, it is an ugly tie. In fact, it is the ugliest one I own. All the others are at the cleaners and I am required to wear a tie to work, so today is ugly tie day. What furniture can I help you find?"

Completely thrown off and smiling against her best efforts not to, the woman admitted she was searching for a dining room set. Brett took her to the dining room set area and acknowledged her fear. "I know you don't want someone hovering over you while you shop, I'll wait over there. When you're ready to purchase or if you have a question just wave at me, and I'll come right back. Otherwise, I'll leave you alone. My name is Brett." He sold her a six piece dining room set. Two weeks later, she came back and bought a pair of recliners and a four piece bedroom set for her daughter.

Make Solutions

When faced with a challenge you have a choice: make an excuse or make a solution. Brett remained calm when faced with a problem, recognized the core issue, and found a quality solution for his situation. He made light of himself in the face of an insult and then openly addressed the real issue – the customer did not want a sales person stalking her the entire time she was shopping. When faced with a problem, figure out the underlying issue so you can address the problem instead of covering it with an excuse.

This choice of making a solution or making an excuse applies when we are confronted with external problems as well as when we deal with our own internal problems. Often when people tell me about a situation they are facing, and specifically ask for advice or possible solutions, I find they are resistant to all suggestions. Instead, they seem to enjoy practicing all their excuses out loud. For example, I once had a friend ask me about solving her dry skin issues. We agreed on a good brand of lotion, but she claimed she could never find the time to apply it. She didn't want to apply it after a shower because she hated the feeling of lotion when she got dressed. She didn't want to apply it before bed because she didn't want the feeling of lotion on the sheets. She didn't have time to wait for the lotion to absorb, and did not have any other time of the day when she could conveniently apply it. She seemed satisfied when I was stumped and could not come up with a solution which was acceptable to her. (I did not know about non-greasy formulas back then.)

We do what we practice, so stop practicing excuses. Start thinking of, trying out, and accepting solutions. Not every possible solution will work, but it is better to try and fail than to do nothing. When faced with a difficult situation I like to think of my very loving and totally no nonsense granny. She would have had a reply for any excuse I tried and would have tolerated nothing less than hard work and personal responsibility. If I would have told her I really wanted to learn to speak a foreign language but just could not find the time, she would have immediately called me out for watching TV instead of studying. When an excuse comes to mind, direct your energy toward creating and testing a potential solution instead of creating supporting arguments for your excuse.

Shake-Up: Take a Cold Shower

Are you already coming up with an excuse for not taking a cold shower instead of creating a solution? Taking a cold shower sounds miserable, but it really isn't. The benefits of taking cold showers include increased circulation, improved immunity, increased alertness, and reduced depression. It can help calm your frustration and stimulate your brain. Here's a little help with a solution for completing this Shake-Up. If stepping into a cold shower seems like too much of a shock, start with a warm shower and then slowly decrease the temperature.

Day 23

Schooled

I used to work for an afterschool program. When our director chose to pursue a new career, one of the site coordinators and I decided to start our own company and take over running the program. We had spoken to the superintendent of the school district and had several meetings in his office about this plan. The thing I remember most about his office – other than it being much too small for meetings – was the sign on his desk that read, "Always Make New Mistakes." During our meetings the superintendent had agreed that the transition for the students and parents would be smooth since we were planning to run the new program in the same style as the current program. It seemed as if everyone was on board.

Involved in these meetings had been representatives from the city who ran a similar program with the parks department. The plan as I understood it was for them to supplement our program with sports activities and games run by their staff just as they had in the past. We spent the summer setting up the company structure, writing curriculum, and interviewing and hiring staff so we would be ready to go when the school year started. Every couple of weeks we would ask the superintendent to sign off on the program so we could access the grant funding and start purchasing supplies, but he never did. About two weeks before school started we really needed to order supplies, so we pressed for a response. We then received an email stating the school district would not be choosing us to run their afterschool program this school year. Instead, they would have the city run the entire program and we should clear out. When we called the superintendent, intending to ask, "What the heck?" the answer we got from his secretary was he was out of town, on vacation, in the mountains, and could not be reached.

Make New Mistakes

How cowardly was this man? He couldn't tell us to our faces he was not going to allow us to run the program? We were certainly a couple of tough ladies but not particularly intimidating. Looking back, we realized the people over at the city had known the whole time. They had meetings with us and pretended to write down dates and times for events, class schedules, and future meetings, all the while they were smugly planning to run the program themselves. Simply telling us the truth two months earlier would have saved us and so many others so much frustration. We spent the entire summer preparing and we had about 60 people ready to start working.

All of those people could have been out finding other jobs had they known we would not be able to provide one.

sigh Sometimes we fail. It's ok. It happens. If you fail make sure you know you did everything you could to succeed. You didn't make an excuse. You didn't blame someone else. You gave it your all and you still didn't win. Learn from the mistake, forgive yourself, and go make new mistakes.

Shake-Up: Try Something New

The painting class you have been rescheduling. A new restaurant you keep staring into every time you pass by. Whatever it is, stop making up reasons to put it off and try something new. What you choose might not work out. You may discover you hate painting or the restaurant is revolting, but you will have tried. Even if an experience turns out to be a terrible disaster, at least you had the experience. Having an experience gives you an opportunity to learn and to grow. Doing nothing gives you nothing, but a chance for regret.

Day 24

Next Please

Out of breath from running to the building from where she parked the car, Lata pushed through the post office door to mail a package just 10 minutes before closing. She considered standing in line for the counter, but it was a long line. She decided to stand in line at the self-service machine instead since there was only one person using the machine and one other person in line. Miscalculation! The woman using the machine continued to produce a parade of envelopes from her bag and repeated the postage process for each one. While Lata was waiting, and eyeing the counter line, a man got in the self-service line behind her. Now Lata was experiencing the classic line dilemma. Stay in the self-serve line and wait or switch to the counter line which appeared, at least for the moment, to be moving? The man behind her switched lines and Lata followed. After a few moments in the counter line the man turned to her and invited her to go in front of him. He said she was in front in the other line and should be in front in this line.

Refocus

Lata was shocked and happy. It is amazing how much joy we can bring to someone's life just by being a decent person. Mystery man wasn't required to allow her to go in front of him, but he did, and it made her day. Refocus yourself on what is happening around you instead of only what is going on in your own life. Check in with your friends and your family. Try to be kind and patient toward those around you. Refocus and start seeing the larger picture instead of only one piece of the puzzle.

Shake-Up: Go for a Walk

I have yet to find a simpler way to clear my head. A little fresh air, some time outside in nature, and suddenly the rest of the day seems like something I can handle. Go for a walk and try to notice something you haven't noticed before. Maybe a neighbor replanted their garden. Perhaps a new shop is opening in a previously vacant building. The walk doesn't need to be long. Use it as an opportunity to shift your focus away from your daily life and observe others and your surroundings.

Day 25

Dull, Interrupted

When Sarah first enrolled her daughter in ballet classes she went to the local dance supply store to look for the required tights, leotard, and shoes. She hated shopping in retail stores, but she needed the items before the class started the next day. When Sarah entered the store the woman at the desk looked up at her as if Sarah had just answered her cell phone in the middle of a quiet theater during the third act. Sarah smiled hesitantly and started looking around. She couldn't find tights in her daughter's size, so she went over to the counter to ask for help. The answer? A very terse, "No, we're out." Sarah left the store, but didn't give up. Later, she found all she needed at a local consignment shop.

The next night Sarah was chatting with one of the other parents while their kids were in class, and they got to talking about how hard it was to find the required dance clothes. When she mentioned the store she visited first, his response was, "I've been in there several times and they are the coldest bunch of people I have ever met."

Find a Happy

We might have thought to dismiss the salesperson's attitude as her having one bad day, but it seemed as though Sarah's experience was not a fluke. Other parents were having the same experience at different times. Clearly, the woman working in the store was not happy. If you're going to have a job working with people, you should like working with people. If you must do something you do not enjoy try to find the bright side, like a fun co-worker or an employee discount. If there isn't one and you can't switch jobs just yet, think about something which makes you happy while you get the job done. Your unhappiness comes across in your manner every day without you noticing, even though everyone else does. Joy and positivity also come across in your manner without you noticing. Choose something to be happy about. It could be a hobby, a friend, or the knowledge a 3-day holiday weekend is forthcoming. Let the happiness fill you and override any anger or frustration. Life isn't all sunshine and roses. That's just reality. However, with practice we can teach ourselves to look for the positives around us and see the opportunities for joy in our daily lives.

Shake-Up: List 5 Happies

List five (5) things which make you truly happy and bring joy to your life. My list included hanging out with my family and dressing up in costume. (Seriously, I might have more costumes than regular clothes. Every time someone has a party I immediately start wondering if there is a theme, and if I should wear a costume.) Your list should include anything that brings you joy. Perhaps you love cooking, or reading, or visiting theme parks. If you are having trouble thinking of things which make you happy, try thinking of something you are grateful for. When you are finished with your list save it with your other lists until you reach Day 30. You're so close now!

Part 6

Stand Up

Kindness and compassion are sometimes interpreted as weakness by those who do not understand them. Being compassionate towards someone who is being unkind to you requires much more inner strength than being cruel. It takes strength of character to stand up for yourself and for others. Standing up does not always have to be a battle. You can make a stand with the smallest gesture. Decide to let go of the fear of doing what you know is right. Stand up and become the best you can. Better than you thought you could be.

Day 26

Little Things

When Darren and Tori moved into the house next door to Josh and Edie they had no idea how wonderful their new neighbors would turn out to be. Right from the beginning, Josh and Edie introduced themselves with a plate of food. They would invite Darren, Tori, and their kids over every time they had a family party and they always sent them home with leftovers. If Darren accidentally left the garage door open at night, Josh would walk over and let him know. If Tori was carrying in a carload of groceries Edie would send her son to help. Sometimes Josh would mow both front lawns instead of just his own. Inspired by the hospitality of their neighbors, Darren and Tori soon reciprocated by sending their own plates of food and desserts next door, mowing both lawns, receiving packages when needed, and feeding the cat when their neighbors were on vacation.

Practice Kindness

Kindness spreads. If Josh and Edie would have kept to themselves and only waved once in awhile their new neighbors would have done the same. Instead they took the opportunity to be kind and it paid off. Both sets of neighbors gained friends. We do what we practice and the skills we practice are the ones we improve. Practicing kindness does not have to be complicated. Simply help someone when you see they need it or give them something they were not expecting. Watch out for others instead of walking on by, and do not be afraid to stand on the side of what is right.

Shake-Up: Interact

Try to strike up a conversation with someone you don't know or someone you don't know well. It is usually easier than you think. Talk about the weather if you can't think of anything else and be sure to tune in to possible opportunities. For example, while walking at the state fair I overheard a group of women harassing one of the ladies in their group for being the only one who had not seen anyone she knew when they all had. I stepped in and said, "I can help with that!" I held out my hand and introduced myself. She looked kinda confused so I added, "What's your name?" She answered, "Whitney." I told her, "Problem solved. Now you've seen someone you knew at the fair." The other ladies laughed. As I walked away I heard one of them say, "That was really cool."

Most people are really cool if you treat them well; don't be afraid to interact a bit. Practicing quality communication skills can help you build your confidence and improve your current relationships. Listening to many different people has helped me learn to pick up on subtle cues being given by those around me. Find a way to interact with someone and see how it makes both of you feel.

Day 27

Head Chef

After working as a chef for 25 years, Martin was five days away from opening his own restaurant when he got a phone call. His son had been in a car accident and was in the hospital. His daughter-in-law told him the doctors were fairly confident his son would recover and he didn't have to come. They all knew how much time, money, and effort he had invested in his restaurant; she did not want him to miss opening night. Martin called his sous chef and they met for several hours reviewing the menu and the long list of tasks to be completed before opening. He left his sous chef with the phone numbers of his two closest friends and instructions to call them in the morning for help. Martin packed a bag and spent the rest of the night driving the 386 miles to see his son.

Stay Focused

Martin knew what was important to him and what his priorities were. He knew how terrible it would be if his son took a turn for the worst and he was not by his side. He knew even though his daughter-in-law was trying to sound strong on the phone she needed support and someone to help with the kids while she was at the hospital. Even with money from investors, his reputation as a chef, and his dream on the line, the choice to go to his injured son was one he made almost instantly and without regret.

When you know where your priorities lie, seemingly tough decisions become easier. When you do not know what your priorities are and you are continuously trying to split yourself between two or more important parts of your life, you end up feeling frustrated or guilty most of the time. Martin's priority was his son and family. Upon hearing their son was stable, someone else might have chosen to stay for opening night, get updates over the phone, and drive up a few days later. Allow yourself to be honest with the inner you and the people closest to you about what really matters in your heart. When you follow your priorities, you know you have made the right choice and those layers of guilt and frustration are lifted. Listen to yourself. Focus on what is important to you and start structuring your life so your priorities are being met.

Shake-Up: Make Contact

Call, text, or email someone you care about but haven't spoken to in a while. Listen to their stories and share some of your own. Talking to someone who is a bit removed from your day to day reality can help you take a step back and look critically at what is currently happening in your life. Sometimes when I do this the person on the other end of the line provides a new perspective, and just through the act of sharing my story I start to feel like things are more manageable. Other times I just listen to their stories. After hearing about what they are going through and helping with their problems, I can reevaluate my own situation and determine what I should do next.

Day 28

Best Man

Devon and Avery got married on a budget. Their ceremony was in a park and their reception was held in a community center. They enlisted friends to help with setup and running the show, and even though it was well planned, they were worried they had overlooked something. Usually, they were the ones who ran events for others. They did not have someone lined up to be in charge of their event. Fortunately, their friend Mason who's only assigned tasks were to help decorate and walk Avery's mother down the isle, saw the need for a master of ceremonies and simply started filling the role without being asked. He had always seemed like such a laid-back type of guy who usually didn't get involved in complicated tasks. Instead of his usual ways he totally stepped it up and ran everything from the announcements, to the toast, to the bouquet toss. Devon and Avery were grateful and amazed.

Engage

Devon and Avery never knew if Mason was simply having a good day and wanted to be helpful or if he was trying to pay them back for the two months they let him live with them after he lost his job. They did know they would be forever touched by all of the hard work Mason put into their wedding. The wedding would not have run as calmly or as smoothly without his help.

Mason could have kept his job simple and walked Avery's mother down the isle as he was asked, then bailed. Instead he volunteered to help with setup, took it upon himself to figure out what needed to be done, and did it without being asked. When you see something needs to happen it is time to engage. It does not matter if the act is small or if you think you might not make a difference. Even a seemingly insignificant act to one can make a world of difference to another. Devon and Avery didn't see Mason much after their wedding, but they always remembered his impact, and were always grateful for his effort. Take the opportunity to come to someone's defense when they are being picked on, or to help a friend in their hour of need. Be present and engage in what is happening around you and not just in your own world. You may never know how much of an impact you make in someone's life when you engage. You may turn their bad day into a good day. You might stop them from yelling at their children when they get home because you let them share your umbrella at the bus stop. Engaging with others should be a lifelong commitment to bettering society every time you have the opportunity.

Shake-Up: Surprise Someone

Lift someone up with a little surprise. Pay for their coffee, give a small gift, show up and visit. Do something for someone else without them asking and see how it lifts both of you.

Day 29

Fine Artist

When Rachel was little she was always drawing. She would try to draw almost everything she saw. Even playing outside when the other kids would be making up games or riding their bikes, Rachel would be drawing with chalk or drawing in the dirt with a stick. When asked what she wanted to be when she grew up, she would say she wanted to be an artist. She started to notice adults would make a bit of an odd smile and hesitantly say things like, "Oh, that's nice." One evening she showed her mother a picture she had been drawing all day and announced she was going to be an artist when she grew up. Her mother became annoyed and told her, "Artists never amount to anything. Do something useful with your life and become a doctor." Rachel was uncertain about this. The next time she was asked what she wanted to be when she grew up she answered, "A doctor" just as a test. The response was overwhelming. Every time she said she wanted to be a doctor adults would smile and tell her how smart she was and how becoming a doctor was an excellent career choice.

Sixty years later, after retiring from a career in medicine, Rachel was going through boxes in her attic. She found an old sketch book and fondly remembered how much she had loved to draw. As she flipped through the pages she also realized she had been pretty good at it. Deciding there was no time like the present; Rachel enrolled in art classes at the local community college and began a new career as an artist.

Encourage

Someone else's dream may not sound sensible to us. It might seem crazy or useless, but their dream is important to them.

Rachel's mother and the other adults around her discouraged Rachel from following her passion. Encourage others to follow their dreams and encourage yourself to do the same. You may have to work a "day job" to keep the lights on, but you can still make progress towards your personal goals. Do not allow others to hold you back or convince you your dream is unworthy.

Shake-Up: List 5 Wishes

Make a list of five (5) wishes for yourself. These could be things you want to do, get, fix, make, build, have, see, experience. Anything you really, truly want. It might be something simple which has been nagging you for years like wanting to finally finish the half-pieced quilt in your closet. It could be to conquer your fear of flying and travel to a different country. Maybe you want to run a half-marathon or learn to speak another language. When writing this book, I wrote my own list of five wishes. I wrote my list mid-May. By the end of October I had accomplished three of my wishes and had plans in place for how I was going to accomplish the other two. It is amazing what you can accomplish when you are focused and have the right tools and the right attitude. Write your five wishes and save them with your other lists. Tomorrow we bring them all together.

Day 30

Box of Chocolates

When I was in elementary school, our school would have at least one fundraiser each year. They always had amazing looking boxes of candies, cookies, and chocolates. When I was about 10 years old, I decided to use my hard earned allowance to buy a box of rose-shaped chocolates. When the box came, I was so satisfied. I had wanted one of those boxes for years and I finally had one. I put the box in my closet and took it out almost daily to have a look. I would imagine how wonderful those chocolates were going to taste when I finally opened the box. I loved the fact they were all mine and I would not have to share with anyone. Over the course of a few weeks I forgot to take the box out every day and I only took it out once every few days. After awhile longer, I only took it out every few weeks. I would run my fingers over the contours of the rose shapes on the top, and imagine how special it was to have the tasty box of chocolates all to myself.

About three years later when I was cleaning out my closet, I uncovered the box of rose-shaped chocolates on the top shelf. I had completely forgotten about them and was surprised and delighted to find the box. Within a few excited moments I had removed all the plastic and carefully lifted the lid. My heart sank as removing the cushioned insert revealed a box of tiny chocolate roses covered in some sort of a white film. Convincing myself that they were probably still ok to eat, I took a long awaited bite and spit it out. Crumbly and dry, the chocolate roses had sat in the top of the closet for so long my lovely treats were no longer edible.

Get It

More on my chocolates in a bit. You made it to Day 30! Go get those lists.

You now have six lists of five items each which you wrote down during the various Shake-Ups throughout the book. Three of these lists contain your goals. Let's start with the Never Minds. This list is your first set of goals. It contains five things you want to give up, remove, or release from your life. These are things which bother you, annoy you, or hold you back, and you want to stop thinking about them, stop worrying about them, and never mind about them again. Give yourself permission to let go of the five things on this list.

The next list of goals is your list of five Happies. Review your list. Your happies are the things you love. This is what you should be enjoying as often as possible. When you have a decision to make about what to do or which path to take, you can refer to this list to help you decide which option will move you toward happiness. If you make doing what you wrote on this list a priority, you will be well on your way.

The third list containing your goals is the Wishes list. Review your list of wishes. Your list of wishes spells out the things you most want to make happen in your life. Achieving your wishes can be a long process, but that's ok. The journey makes the achievement even sweeter. Stay focused on your wishes and work on creating a plan which gets you to your goal. To create the plan you will need tools. Do you know where those tools are? Yep, on the other three lists.

Find the Qualities list and review it. This is your own individual arsenal. These qualities are yours, and no one can take them away from you unless you let them. Whenever you start to doubt yourself refer to this list and remember how special and capable you are. You'll need to use your strengths to achieve your goals from the three goal lists.

Next, find the Relationships page and review the list of people you wrote down. These are your helpers and advisors. They are the ones who will give you good advice and keep you on the right track. They will help you if and when you need it, and get out of your way when you don't. They will be your support system and the base of your network. As much as we might like to think it, none of us can do everything on our own. We will all need help at some point. When you need help, consult this list to know where to turn. If they are not able to guide you, ask these resources if they know someone who can.

Lastly, let's turn to the Positives list. Remember when all those good things happened to you? This list can be like a life raft on a day when you feel nothing is going your way and you are moving in the opposite direction from your goals. When this happens and you start feeling down, review your list of positives and remember all the good in your life. When things are going well and you are having a good day keep adding new events to the Positives list. This will give you an even stronger tool to lift your spirits whenever you need a reminder that good things do happen to you.

If you downloaded the PDF from TheShakeUpBook.com you'll see three of the lists have the letter G inside of a circle in the bottom right corner. This is to help you remember these are the lists of your goals. The other three have the letter T inside of a circle in the bottom right corner to help you remember those are lists of your tools.

I waited on those chocolates because I cherished the *idea* of eating them. When I finally acted, it was too late to enjoy *actually* eating them. Sometimes we get stuck focusing on the idea of all the great things we intend to do instead of getting out there and doing them. We keep making a plan to plan instead of making a plan *and* taking action. We might worry the real thing will not be as good as we expected or we are concerned we might make a mistake. Do not let those worries stop you. Keep going and make adjustments as needed. Quit sitting around waiting for your dream to come to you. Use your tools and go out there and get it.

Shake-Up: Reward Yourself

Congratulations on completing all 30 days! Before you continue your transformation using your new tools, you have one Shake-Up left: reward yourself. I like to set up small rewards for myself which I earn by completing tasks. It doesn't seem to matter if the task is large and the reward is small, I'm always happy to get a little bonus in celebration of my accomplishment. You can use this technique as well to help motivate you to finish tasks and complete goals. Today you finished this book so your Shake-Up is to reward yourself. You earned it.

Follow Through

You did it! You completed The Shake Up. Now it's time to follow through. Your lists are tools you are meant to use. Don't bury them in a drawer. Keep them out where you can use them. Write on them. Edit them. Make notes in the margins. Go back and reread parts of the book as often as you'd like to reinforce your favorite concepts, or try doing the Shake-Ups again in a different way. Your journey toward happiness, harmony, and success continues! If you didn't get the custom PDF form for the lists at the beginning and you would like to get your free copy now it's still available at TheShakeUpBook.com.

Consider gifting this book to a friend and going through the days together. If you couldn't quite muster the courage to complete some of the Shake-Ups the first time around you might be ready to tackle them on the next round with a friend on board to help keep you accountable.

If you would like more resources from me, check out the growing library of blog posts and workshops on my coaching website CamilleDiaz.com. While you're there you can read more about my coaching style and contact me if you think you would like us to work together one-on-one. To connect with me and others who have read *The Shake Up* on social media you can find me @CamUnfiltered. I look forward to hearing from you.

Best wishes,

About the Author

Camille Diaz is a life coach and strategist who helps enterprising people streamline their businesses and find happiness and harmony in their lives. She has become a sounding board and a trusted source of tough love for those looking to calm the chaos and create a better work-life balance. Her ongoing goal is to boost the confidence of others and help each individual reach their personal best.

Camille loves dancing, gardening, and baking pie, though her most underappreciated talent is her ability to neatly fold fitted sheets. She currently lives in Oklahoma with her athletic husband and their two charming daughters.

Websites:

CamilleDiaz.com

TheShakeUpBook.com

Social: @CamUnfiltered

CPSIA information can be obtained
at www.ICGtesting.com
Printed in the USA
FFOW02n2128231017
41451FF